THOMAS FORD MEMORIAL LIBRARY

W9-CFB-399

SEP - - 2015

THOMAS FORD MEMORIAL LIBRARY
800 CHESTNUT
WESTERN SPRINGS, IL 60558

Watch Me Go!

MY RIPSTIK

Victor Blaine

PowerKiDS
press.

New York

THOMAS FORD MEMORIAL LIBRARY

Published in 2015 by The Rosen Publishing Group, Inc.
29 East 21st Street, New York, NY 10010

Copyright © 2015 by The Rosen Publishing Group, Inc.

All rights reserved. No part of this book may be reproduced in any form without permission in writing from the publisher, except by a reviewer.

First Edition

Editor: Sarah Machajewski
Book Design: Mickey Harmon

Photo Credits: Cover, p.1 (helmet) ronstik/Shutterstock.com; cover, pp. 1 (girl), 6 (wave boarding) Sergey Ryzhov/Shutterstock.com; pp. 5 (rider), 10, 18 bunebake/Shutterstock.com; p. 5 (helmet) Fred Sweet/Shutterstock.com; p. 6 (surfing) Logan Carter/Shutterstock.com; p. 9 © iStockphoto.com/Syldavia; p. 13 membio/Thinkstock.com; p. 14 http://en.wikipedia.org/wiki/Caster_board#mediaviewer/File:Wene-160-Skaten.JPG; p. 17 gorillaimages/Shutterstock.com; p. 21 Voyagerix/Shutterstock.com; p. 22 (boy) Digital Media Pro/Shutterstock.com; p. 22 (wave board) http://commons.wikimedia.org/wiki/Category:Caster_boards#mediaviewer/File:Waveboard_total_1.JPG.\.

Library of Congress Cataloging-in-Publication Data

Blaine, Victor.
My ripstik / by Victor Blaine.
p. cm. — (Watch me go!)
Includes index.
ISBN 978-1-4994-0255-1 (pbk.)
ISBN 978-1-4994-0241-4 (6-pack)
ISBN 978-1-4994-0251-3 (library binding)
1. Skateboarding — Juvenile literature. 2. Skateboarding — Technological innovations — Juvenile literature. I. Title.
GV859.8 B53 2015
796.6 —d23

Manufactured in the United States of America

CPSIA Compliance Information: Batch #CW15PK: For Further Information contact Rosen Publishing, New York, New York at 1-800-237-9932

CONTENTS

If you ever want to ride
something cool, try riding
a RipStik!

A RipStik is like a skateboard. Riding one feels like you are **surfing** or snowboarding!

A RipStik is also called a wave board. RipStiks and wave boards are fun ways to exercise.

You stand on a RipStik's **decks**. The decks are big enough to fit your feet.

Each deck has one wheel.
The rider controls one wheel
with each foot.

13

The decks are joined by a bar.
The bar helps the RipStik move.

Riding a RipStik can be hard at first. You may fall off. Wearing a **helmet** keeps you from getting hurt.

After you learn how to ride a RipStik, you can learn to do tricks.

One trick is called a kickflip.
A kickflip is when you spin
your board in the air.

3 1308 00329 4592

Can you do any tricks
on your RipStik?

WORDS TO KNOW

deck · helmet · surfing

INDEX

D
decks, 11, 12, 15

H
helmet, 16

T
tricks, 19, 20, 23

W
wheel, 12

WEBSITES

Due to the changing nature of Internet links, PowerKids Press has developed an online list of websites related to the subject of this book. This site is updated regularly. Please use this link to access the list: www.powerkidslinks.com/wmg/rips